# Walking the Tightrope of Life

### Refuel. Renew. and Re-Center Your Work-Life Demands

# Walking the
# Tightrope of Life
## Refuel. Renew. and Re-Center Your Work-Life Demands

**Sharise M. Nance, LCSW, CCTP**

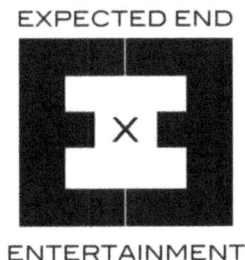

EXPECTED END

ENTERTAINMENT

Atlanta, GA

Published by Expected End Entertainment/EX3 Books
ExpectedEndEntertainment@gmail.com * www.EX3Books.com
**ISBN-10:** 0-9968932-7-X
**ISBN-13:** 978-0-9968932-7-5
Printed in the United States of America

# DEDICATION

This book is dedicated to those who place a cause or belief before their personal needs. The helping profession can appear to be a thankless experience but you find the beauty in assisting individuals through the healing process.

# PRAISE FOR THE BOOK

"A must read for individuals in social services, education, and health care. This book helps us understand how the stress of our work impacts our personal and family lives. Walking the Tightrope is an excellent resource for staff training and workshops by identifying ways to renew and refuel our lives."
**Fredalene Barletta Bowers, Ph.D., Professor, Child Development and Family Relations, Indiana University of Pennsylvania**

"Walking the Tightrope of Life delivers an accessible and important reminder to maintain work-life balance and 'Physician, heal thyself'. ...Though intended for healthcare and helping professionals, the core sentiments in this book are useful for all audiences.
**Abhishek Jain, MD, Board-Certified Physician in Psychiatry, Forensic Psychiatry, and Psychosomatic Medicine.**

To stave off burnout is to acknowledge the necessity of being mindful in establishing a balance between the personal and the professional, between home and the office. Reading this book provides an opportunity for improving our level of happiness and our productivity.
**Beverly J. Goodwin, Ph.D., Professor of Psychology, Indiana University of Pennsylvania**

Walking the Tight Rope of Life will be your resource tool to help you recognize the signs of the stressors in your life (work/home). To become aware of the affect stress has on your overall health, you will then be able to practice good self-care. Hemby-Nance's book asks you those important questions to help you understand those stressors in your life. Once you understand, she helps you on your way with steps to manage your life in a more balanced way.
**Bonita Lee Penn, Editing Manger, Soul Pitt Quarterly Magazine.**

# CONTENTS

# INTRODUCTION

Counselors, teachers, social workers, nurses, protective service workers, psychologists and caregivers are some of the many professionals who consistently give of themselves to improve the quality of lives and oftentimes SAVE the LIVES of so many! Working as a helping professional can bring deep satisfaction and lasting rewards.

There are also times when the work seems challenging, invalidating, and thankless and you may feel ineffective in your role when you don't see the fruits of your labor. Can you recall or identify a current colleague who, because of being overwhelmed, stressed, or that feeling of being spread too thin, views coming to work each morning as a chore? Do you know of a helper who finds him or herself struggling to stay present during a session, growing bored, feeling stagnant or complacent, and not being able to remain focused with a client? Are you a supervisor, manager or director struggling with ways to advocate for your staff? Do you recognize some of the aforementioned qualities in yourself? Walking the Tightrope of Life is a guide designed to assist the helping professional struggling with compassion fatigue and/or burnout to find renewal in their work and to enjoy a healthy work-life balance.

# CHAPTER ONE

## MY PLATE IS FULL

*"Much of the stress that people feel doesn't come from having too much to do. It comes from not finishing what they started."*
*~David Allen*

The work day has ended and you are looking forward to spending a relaxing evening with your family. You've wrapped up the final session of the day with your client and headed out the door. However, the client's transportation has not yet arrived. The client does not have family who can take them home. You are not permitted to transport clients and your conscious will not allow you to leave the client in the lobby waiting area alone. So, you spend nearly two hours waiting with the client until transportation arrives.

During this time, you are working hard to remain present with the client, but you are thinking of the laundry list of tasks in your personal life that are just as important as your current task. You find yourself in a moral dilemma of deciding how long you can stay with your client and wondering how your children will get home from practice. "I should have planned better," is the resounding statement that keeps playing in your mind. Guilt sets in as you question, "Can I continue to sacrifice time with my family and do this work?"

When transportation arrives, your client is moved to tears that you sacrificed your time to make sure she arrived home safe. In this moment, you are reminded of the rewarding part of your work and the lives you touch daily.

Your client arrives home safely, you are relieved

to learn that your mother picked up the children and all is well again as your plate doesn't seem so full. Once you step in the door, your daughter informs you she needs help with a science project due the next day. Your husband was just informed of a mandatory work-related business meeting in the morning (leaving you little to no time to plan the children's transportation to school and you making it to work on time). Laundry is full and dinner still needs prepared. At this moment, it feels as if you go from crisis to crisis unequipped to prepare or manage the sudden events in your personal life. You are at the mercy of a full schedule and everything in your life is too important to remove from the schedule. "My husband needs me. My children need me. I love the work I do and I need the job to contribute to the household. But something has to give!" Does this sound familiar?

How do you balance this plate full of spouse, parent, and helping professional as the main entrée every day? With these three courses, some days it may seem your plate is piled so high it resembles a small mountain. Even when the metaphoric pieces of food are close to falling off the plate, you find room for each serving as you are fulfilled by each portion. Yet, the question remains, how can I keep this up on a regular basis?

Being overbooked and overburdened has become far too common in the helping profession. Some of us may ask ourselves if these experiences are prerequisites for entering the helping profession. Having a full plate and not being able to give one area the attention it needs on a regular basis can lead to guilt, compassion fatigue, and/or cynicism.

**Keeping a healthy balanced schedule of work and personal balance in my life.**

We will focus more on work-life balance in a later chapter. The following reflection questions will assist you in balancing your plate.

What are some triggers that inform you that you may not be able to handle your "full plate?"

_____
_____
_____.

What does a typical day look like for you?

_____
_____
_____.

Who can I ask for help when I am feeling overwhelmed?

_____
_____
_____.

When was the last time I took vacation time?

_____

_____

_____.

*Tips to stop feeling overwhelmed by your full schedule:*

**RUN THE DAY:** "Either you run the day or the day runs you." Running the day requires that we find ways that work for us to get organized. Disorganization is a key ingredient to feeling overwhelmed, having a full plate and ultimately allowing the day to pull you by the collar into the next task.

**GOAL LIST vs TO DO LIST:** If you fail to plan, you are planning to fail. Set the tone for the entire day by being prepared. What are the most important goals I need to accomplish today? Many of us are guilty of adding a laundry list of items to a daily "To Do" list that rarely get completed. A few years ago, LinkedIn.com released a survey that stated 90% of professionals admitted they're unable to accomplish all the tasks on To Do lists by the end of an average work day. For example, do you really need to list tasks such as: grocery shopping, laundry, pick up kids from daycare? You will remember to do these tasks anyway, as they are a part of your routine. Instead of

WALKING THE TIGHTROPE OF LIFE

flooding those lists, focus on goals you want to accomplish for the day.

When waking up each morning or before you go to bed at night, think of the "1-3-5 rule." On any given day, assume you can only accomplish 1 big goal, 3 medium goals and/or 5 small goals. If you find this to be too overwhelming, revise to fit your schedule. 1-3-5 gives you the power to prioritize, choose what gets done, run the day and you are less likely to get burned out from unnecessary tasks.

**STOP DOING EVERYONE'S WORK:** This might be a difficult concept for those with "Type A" personalities to grasp. "I'll do it" and "If you want anything done right, you have to do it yourself" are common statements and beliefs held by "Type A's." Or, you may be part of a team and want to be a "good team player" by taking on the workload of your co-workers. Yes, teamwork makes the dream work. As a responsible teammate, you owe it to yourself and teammates to say no (discussed in a later chapter) and inform them when your caseload is too high or you are spread too thin. Doing it all exhausts your potential for greatness. Doing everything depletes you and you cannot give to others from an empty well. Lean on your resources and remember it is not the role of any helping professional to do it all; we must collaborate.

**BREATHE:** Breathing is so automatic that many of us are unable to take the time to focus on our breathing, especially in stressful situations. Deep breathing has many benefits such as the promotion of better blood flow, releasing toxins from the body and aiding in better sleep. Breathing calms the reactive part of our brains. Imagine having your favorite cup of coffee or tea in front of you. Now inhale deeply to take in the aroma. Exhale as if you're blowing on the hot beverage to cool it off. You have just completed a great deep breathing exercise to begin the day or to use when you are feeling overwhelmed.

**WHAT CHANGES CAN YOU MAKE TODAY?** As creatures of habit, we are comfortable in our daily routines. It takes great discipline to maintain a daily routine. However, it is quite difficult to recognize when the routine is no longer effective and change is needed. If your current routine is adding stress, how can you lighten the load? Do you consistently overbook your days? What tasks can you delegate or outsource? Sometimes, a minor tweak in our routines can be the change we need to help us find more balance in our lives. (We will discuss life balance in a later chapter).

Remember, there are many expectations placed on helping professionals throughout the course of the day. It is unrealistic to meet every expectation and it may not be in the best interest of you or the clients you serve to try to meet all of them. However, we owe it to ourselves, the clients we serve and the profession to practice good self-care. This self-care may include a vacation from our responsibilities, without the guilt!

Be kind to you and whatever is good for your soul…do that!

# CHAPTER TWO

## LIFE BALANCE = SATISFACTION

*"Balance is better time management, energy management and boundary management. Balance means making choices and enjoying these choices." ~Sharise M. Nance*

"Never get too busy making a living that you forget to make a life" is a quote that comes to mind when I reflect on the many sacrifices made by helping professionals. Most, if not all, of us are in pursuit of balance in our lives. Balance is important as it helps us to compartmentalize the various areas of our lives. A common trend in the helping profession is the struggle to find balance in one's professional and personal life. Frontline workers and first responders are consistently faced with the privilege and challenge of directly impacting lives. How do helping professionals disconnect from such an emotionally charged task and enjoy their personal lives? How effective will you be in affecting change if you find your personal life in shambles? I have heard many of my colleagues comment that helping professionals' personal lives have to be stress free in order to be effective in this work. How realistic is a life free of stress and difficult situations? Life is a series of situations as you are either entering a situation, in the midst of a situation or exiting a situation. The common denominator in each scenario is YOU and your ability to manage these situations. We are assuming the role of helper and to administer quality help, we must begin by helping ourselves.

What "tools" or skills do you use when you find

you are under stress? What area of your life consistently brings you the most stress? What area of your life consistently brings you the most joy? The demands from both our personal and professional life can make finding balance seem like an impossible goal. With that being said, what do most professionals want out of work-life balance? If you ask several people, you are likely to receive several different answers. In my experiences, I have learned that most people want at least two things from their personal and professional lives: achievement and enjoyment. What is the purpose of "Life Balance" without satisfaction? Satisfaction is typically derived from a sense of achievement and enjoyment of life. However, most people struggle to obtain either. Some of us may find ourselves working 60-70 hours per week and not feeling a sense of achievement and enjoyment. When this occurs, we must stop and ask ourselves, "Why?" What are you hoping to accomplish as a result of working long hours? Are you keeping your end in mind? When we struggle to connect with our "why" in relation to work, our personal lives will suffer. This struggle makes it difficult to find balance and satisfaction in both facets of our lives. Connecting with our "why" allows for the balance to stay true to our values and principles while walking in our life's purpose.

Life balance is not necessarily a 50/50 split. It does not require us to find an equal balance of scheduling an equal number of hours for our work and personal activities. Work-life balance is the proper prioritizing between career and lifestyle (health, pleasure, family, and spirituality/religion). This balance will vary over time. The most effective balance looks different for everyone. The best balance when you are single may change when you have a family. The best balance for your situation today may change tomorrow. Remember, we are not striving for perfection, but searching for the tools to combine a sense of achievement and enjoyment in our careers and personal lives.

My fellow helping professionals are always on my mind. So many helping professionals experience burnout early in their careers from issues that could have been prevented had they been identified and addressed. In an effort to enhance the lives of those in the helping profession, I recently conducted an anonymous survey via social media to capture the work-life balance of 100 helping professionals between the ages of 25-64 years who have been practicing between 0-20+ years. The survey targeted the age, gender, occupation, years of experience, the most difficult task to let go of at the end of the day, and recommendations for enhancing the helping profession.

**The results revealed:**
**Gender**: 90% of the respondents were female and 10% were male.

**Age:** 20% of respondents were between 25-34 years; 51% of respondents were between 35-44 years; 20%

of the respondents were between 45-64 years; and 9% were between 55-64 years.

**Occupation:** 31% Social workers; 8.08% Case Managers; 28.28% Counselors; 2.02% Healthcare Practitioners; 4.04% Healthcare Support Occupations; 1.01% Protective Service Occupations; 1.01% Personal Care and Service Occupations; and 24% identified other professions (Teacher, Career Counselor, Mental Health Advocate, In Home Assessor, Social Work Director, Workforce Development, Community Development, Licensed Behavioral Health Reviewer, Mental Health/Intellectual Disorder Supervisor, Dietician, Patient Advocate, Financial Services, Clinical Director, Life Coach, Psychotherapist, Marriage and Family Therapist, Play Therapist, Family Development Specialist, Clergy).

Years of experience: 26% had 0-5 years; 25% had 5-10 years; 39% had 10-20 years; and 10% had 20+ years of experience.

**What do you have the most difficulty letting go of at the end of your work day?**
50.51%: Incomplete documentation
25.25%: Difficult sessions
10.1%: Lack of or insufficient supervision
21.21%: Difficulty disconnecting from daily routine
11.11%: Other (Unsure, personal stressors, none of the above, taking unfinished work home, difficulties with administration, insufficient resources to do job,

unresolved differences with clients, corporate mistreatment, the families and their issues, resistance from clients, clients who are hard to reach, ineffective administration, under staffed and over-worked, minimal compensation for extra labor)

**What would you like to see enhanced in the helping profession?**
29%: Increased paid time off
14%: Increased paid training
23%: Full tuition reimbursement
2%: Adequate travel reimbursement or company car for travel
2%: Updated equipment to perform daily job responsibilities
13%: The process for advancement and promotions.
27%: Other (Mentorship/support groups, increased pay for all workers, 8-12 weeks maternity paid time off, improved processes, more efficient and consistent support for the professionals who are providing support, higher pay, mental health days, professionalism and caring, student loan forgiveness in all practice areas).

These results are probably not surprising and may even seem familiar to you. The purpose of sharing these results with you was to give you a snapshot of some of the daily struggles you may share with your colleagues. One of the most effective ways to enhance the helping profession is creating metrics from the people who are doing the work to bridge the gaps between the problems and the solutions.

Take a few moments and reflect on what you would like to see changed in the helping profession that would enhance and prolong the quality of the services you provide.

_____

_____

_____

_____

_____

_____

_____

Are you struggling with some of the aforementioned topics? Are you witnessing a trend of the aforementioned topics amongst some of your colleagues or staff? If so, contact me at vitaminchealing@gmail.com to set up a free consultation.

Remember, you deserve to be heard!

# CHAPTER THREE

## LET GO OF GUILT

*"Guilt is to the spirit what pain is to the body."*
*~Elder David Bednar*

Guilt is often an unwelcomed guest in the areas of our lives we seek balance. As helping professionals, having too much guilt leaves us vulnerable to manipulation, depression and weak personal boundaries. Some of the most common "guilt statements" shared amongst helping professionals include:

- I feel guilty because I work long hours and spend less time with family.
- I feel guilty because life has forced me to devote more time to my personal life and less time to work.
- I feel guilty because I missed a friend or family member's event.
- I feel guilty because I chose sleep over completing another task.
- I feel guilty saying no to others!

That final statement is the most common guilt statement. By no means am I implying that guilt is completely bad. Guilt can be a sign that you want to be better and you want more. There is always room for improvement. It is healthy to strive for being a better you each day and to hold yourself accountable. Sometimes, a little guilt can be the fuel you need to make changes. However, when you find yourself consistently feeling guilty for wanting to say no, needing to take a day off, wanting to treat yourself and wanting to enjoy life, it may be time to evaluate your level of self-compassion. When you are consumed with guilt and allow guilt to dictate your every move, you become "guilty" of living in guilt.

As helping professionals, many of us may find ourselves attempting to discern between the types of guilt that allows us to do what is right by our clients without overstepping our boundaries and the guilt that keeps both us and our clients stuck.

The following questions will assist you in processing what takes place within you when you find yourself battling guilt.

When do you feel guilty?

_____
_____
_____.

Are you more concerned with how you will appear to others or worried that others will think less of you if you do something or fail to do something?

_____
_____
_____
_____.

How often do you find yourself on the receiving end of a guilt trip from someone who is attempting to use guilt as a weapon?

_____
_____
_____.

What purpose does it serve to hold on to the guilt?

_____

_____

_____.

These tips can help you reframe the way you view self-guilt:

1. **Get in wise mind.** Guilt is an emotion and emotions are important in certain situations (loving our spouses, children, showing remorse, having compassion). Getting in wise mind is the medium between reason and emotion. Wise mind is based off your life experiences and what you know to be true. The next time you are feeling overwhelmed with guilt, ask yourself, "What would wise mind say?"

2. **Say Yes to You.** When you say yes to everything and everyone else, you are saying no to someone very important – YOU! Feeling guilty for saying no to a request may be perceived as "selfish." Allow me to explain. Someone asks you to do something or invites you to an event and for whatever reason you want to decline. But your guilt will not allow you to decline so you say yes to a request and no to yourself. Remember, no one is going to feel guilty for taking from you so don't you dare feel guilty for taking care of you. I discuss this concept at length in a later chapter.

3. **Use Guilt for Insight Only.** Why do you feel

guilty? What changes can you make? If you feel you have genuinely done something wrong, focus on the lesson and allow it to motivate you to embrace being better.

4.  **Apologize, Accept and Let It Go.** What purpose does the guilt serve in your life? How is your guilt helping your current situation? If you have done something wrong to someone, apologize and let it go. If someone is not ready to accept your apology, accept this as a part of their healing process. Allow them the time and space they need and work toward letting it go. Your guilt will not help the situation.

Do not put yourself on trial and render a "guilty verdict" for every decision you make. Remember, self-compassion and self-guilt cannot co-exist. It is impossible to truly take care of yourself while feeling guilty for taking care of yourself.

# CHAPTER FOUR

## SAY YES TO ME

*"Half of the troubles of this life can be traced by saying yes too quickly and not saying no soon enough." ~Josh Billings*

It's Monday and you are already looking forward to the invitation from your friend to happy hour on Friday. As the week winds down, you are exhausted from work. On the day of the happy hour event, you decide that a quiet evening relaxing at home may be a better choice for your mental and emotional well-being. However, you do not want to say no to your friends, or even worse, disappoint them. You are faced with the dilemma of saying no to your friends or saying yes to you.

How many times have you been faced with the aforementioned scenario? As helping professionals, we often struggle with the guilt of saying yes to ourselves professionally and personally. From a professional standpoint, it appears helping professionals "get paid to care". Having compassion and empathy are probably amongst the reasons many of us chose this field. We can show empathy and set boundaries by knowing when to say no to our clients and yes to us. After all, most of our clients struggle with setting boundaries and as professionals we are charged with modeling the importance of setting boundaries, starting with an emphasis on self-care.

Attending to the needs of others in this profession calls for a response, but this does not mean we must give an immediate "yes". Take the time to reflect on your options. Do not be afraid to say, "I will get back to you later", or "No!" If you know the answer is no, just say no. Why are you apologizing for a request you are unable to fulfill? More importantly, why are you apologizing for saying yes to you? Oftentimes, you are more respected by saying no instead of saying yes to please others. When you say no, you show you are not afraid of admitting that you value your time and you do not have time for everything. Saying yes to you is to be a friend to yourself first. If you live your life depending on other people's approval, you will never feel free and truly happy. Remember, you cannot be all things to all people.

The favorite two-letter word of all 2-year-olds is NO. Try asking a 2-year-old anything and 99.9% of the time, the answer will be no. While we were taught as children to be kind, considerate and to treat others the way you want to be treated, somehow the freedom to say no unapologetically without fear from the public's disapproval got lost. "No" is an option available to you and you have the right to say it. Trying to make other people happy at the expense of your own happiness is a high price to pay. Sometimes, saying no to others is the greatest gift you can give yourself. Saying yes to you is the foundation of self-love. People treat us how we teach them to treat us. Consistently saying no to you sends the message that you don't value yourself. This can lead to resentment, frustration, anger and/or depression.

Before you hesitantly say no to you and yes to someone else's request, ask yourself:

Is saying yes worth it?

_____

_____

Will I have any regrets in making this decision?

_____

_____

Am I holding true to my values?

_____

_____

Are you at peace with yourself and your decisions?

_____

_____

Tips for saying 'No':
- ✓ **Be direct!** "No, I cannot." "No, I do not want to."
- ✓ **Be unapologetic!** No need to make excuses or give tons of reasons.
- ✓ **Don't lie!** Lying leads to guilt and loss of trust.
- ✓ **Practice saying No!**
- ✓ **Don't say, "I'll think about it" if the answer is no.** This process will prolong the inevitable and lead to more stress and guilt.
- ✓ **Saying no does not make you a horrible person, bad friend, family member, spouse, social worker, nurse, case manager, etc.**

Learning to say no is a process and we must remember to be patient and kind to ourselves. Each day, I challenge you to do one thing to say yes to you. As this becomes a part of your daily regimen, notice how you shift from feeling trapped, guilty, angry, and resentful to feeling freer, empowered, and in control of YOUR life.

Say yes to you. You deserve it!

# CHAPTER FIVE

## SEEKING HELP WHEN FACING YOUR FEARS

*"Not everything that is faced can be changed, but nothing can be changed until it is faced."*
~James Baldwin

Ten years ago, I faced my fears and decided to accept a position as a Family Therapist. For so many years in the helping profession, my role was to link children and families to services that would improve their quality of life. I had always admired therapists as they spent time sitting with people and their fears, vulnerabilities, pain, successes and failures. More importantly, they played an intricate role in effecting change in their lives.

I remember being scared out of my mind before meeting with my first mother-daughter family as a therapist. I remember asking my supervisor how do I respond if mom gets frustrated and asks me, "What do you know, do you have children?" I am thankful that he took the time to process this fear with me. He helped me to understand that our clients need to know that we are competent, confident, compassionate and willing to be in the trenches with them. I realized it didn't matter that I was not a parent and may not have experienced similar trials and tribulations. I would not allow my fears of failing my clients stand in the way of helping them experience success in their lives. I began to live through one of my favorite Maya Angelou quotes: "People don't care how much you know until they know how much you care."

The story is an example that we are not exempt

from fear, pain, adversity, mental distress and all of life's complexities. As helping professionals, we must have a heightened awareness of our well-being. What you fear most will show up "sitting on your couch" in your office if it goes unaddressed. To whom much is given, much is required. As people, in positions of power, we have an ethical responsibility to do no harm. Helping professionals should not provide a service if their own unaddressed or untreated condition blocks their capacity to effectively help their clients. How dare we expect our clients to follow recommendations that we have no intention of practicing (i.e. seeking help for depression, drug and alcohol treatment, grief and loss, regular physical examinations)? Remember, to be a truly competent and integrity-based professional, we must resolve our own issues. Practice the same level of emotional maturity and mental well-being we promote. Do unto yourself as you would want clients to do unto themselves.

Fear is one of the few natural emotions. We are born with two fears: the fear of falling and the fear of loud noises. All other fears are learned responses brought to the child by its environment and taught to the child by its parents. The purpose of natural fear is to build in a bit of caution. Children who are made to feel that fear is not okay, it is wrong to express it, and in fact, that they shouldn't even experience it, will have a difficult time appropriately dealing with their fear as adults.

Fear that is continually repressed becomes panic,

a very unnatural emotion. Perhaps, viewing fear through this lens could explain why many of us struggle with conquering our fears. Facing your fears can be a process and overcoming these fears will happen in its own time. Fear does not have to be a part of who you are.

How committed are you to resolving your own issues?

_____
_____
_____.

How do you handle conflict?

_____
_____
_____.

Do you experience difficulties when working with someone of another race, culture, sex, or religion?

_____
_____
_____.

## ACTIVITY

✓ Make a list of all the people, places, objects and/or situations that you fear.
✓ Arrange this list from the least frightening to the most frightening.
✓ Begin by facing the least frightening fear and practice until the activity feels natural.
✓ After engaging in this activity, reward yourself.

Fear loses its power when discussed openly. Many of us have a fear of failure, loss and even success. Perhaps, the most challenging part of the helping profession is reducing the risk of someone losing their life due to an unsuccessful medical procedure or suicide. Many of us take these losses personal and view them as failed treatment. When I entered the mental health profession, many of my mentors coached me to anticipate clients' suicidal feelings. To date, I have not experienced suicidality of any client and truly believe that if we are practicing ethically, competently and compassionately, no matter the outcome, we will not fail our clients.

How can you face your fears and make a difference in the helping profession?

- Have the courage to hold yourself and your colleagues accountable to maintain the integrity of the profession. Do not be afraid to be a whistleblower. Remember, this cause is bigger than you!

- Do self-reflection often. Assess if you are satisfied with your work and personal life. What are your triggers? What changes can you make today? Do you know when you are overwhelmed?

- Be a mentor or seek mentorship.

- Be specific in identifying your fear(s). What are you afraid of? What is wreaking havoc in your life? What pictures are you creating in your mind? Where do you feel the fear in your body? How do you react to the fear? What triggers this fear? Be an observer of what is going on within you!

- Journaling: After identifying these fears, get them down on paper, which is another strategy of getting this negative energy out. Seeing these fears on paper can help you make sense of them.

- Seek Counseling: Getting an objective perspective and talking through these fears with a licensed professional is another powerful way to assist you in conquering your fears. A professional can help you examine if you have a fear of success or a fear of failure. While therapy can be powerful and even life changing, make sure the therapist is a good fit for you. Remember, we are not exempt. To be a better helper, you must seek help for yourself. Hurting people do hurt people. Our first duty is to do no harm!

- The Now: Be present in the moment. Oftentimes fear comes from past learning experiences and anticipating future failures. You have no control over the past, but you do have control over the present moment. Grounding techniques through breathing is a great way to get back to the present. Try the "4-7-8 Breathing Technique." Place your tongue behind your teeth. Breathe in quietly for 4 seconds, hold for 7 seconds and exhale for 8 seconds.

- Gratitude: Instead of ruminating within your fears, spend that time expressing gratitude. What are you grateful for? If you are fearful of public speaking, be grateful for the opportunity to speak in front of people. If you are fearful of taking a test, be grateful that you have the qualifications to take the test.

- Awareness: Be aware of your thoughts, daily routines and habits. What are you reading? What are you watching? Who are you spending time around? Some ways to combat your fears are to read on your specific fears, watch a motivation video and/or spend time around successful people. Any successful person has overcome some form of fear.

- Nutrition: The food you eat can have a huge impact on how you feel. All the sugars, additives and other chemicals in some foods can have an effect in creating balance in our minds and bodies. Find a balanced diet that works for you and make it a lifestyle.

- Be a verb: The only way out of your fear is through it. The more time we spend ruminating within the fear, the more power we give it. When we take action, we weaken the fear. Thinking will not overcome fear, but action will! Feel the fear and do it anyway.

Everything you want is on the other side of fear, as you traverse through your unique journey to overcoming fear. YOU are the constant in everything that happens or does not happen in your life. Oftentimes, fear is a huge barrier in deciding. How many times have you allowed fear to be the driver while you ride shotgun? You cannot have faith and fear, you must pick one. Remember, the fears we don't face become our limits!

# CHAPTER SIX

## MANAGE YOUR ENERGY AND THEN YOUR TIME

*"Time management is really a misnomer; the challenge is not to manage time but to manage ourselves. ~Stephen R. Covey*

Have you ever sat in a meeting and thought, "This could have been sent in an email or summed up in 30 minutes?" Do you create daily "To Do" lists to manage your time more effectively? Do you find yourself saying, "I have so much to do right now, I can't possibly complete it all today?" If you answered yes to any of the questions, this chapter is dedicated to you.

Time is what we want the most, but often use the worst. While time can be our most valuable asset and a huge liability, energy management is just as, if not more, important. When we are managing energy, we are managing priorities, focus and the people we allow into our space. The hours in the day we choose to invest in both our professional and personal lives must be carefully managed to insure we have the energy available to invest in our highest priorities.

In the *7 Habits of Highly Effective People*, Stephen Covey highlights this concept when he describes how often the 'urgent in our lives' – what seems most demanding in the moment – crowds out the 'important' – priorities that are more consequential but don't require immediate attention.

Take a moment and reflect on the amount of mental and spiritual energy you absorb professionally in a day. You may find yourself in the most rewarding (saving a life, bearing witness to a client making a huge shift from being stuck to unstuck) and daunting situation (removing children from an unsafe environment, a client taking their life). When providing services to individuals with chronic illnesses, severe mental illnesses, children and families; every issue can be deemed urgent. Energy management in these situations is imperative for your self-care and the safety of those you serve. When managing energy, bear in mind "What MUST get done today?" and "What MUST I attend to immediately?" This may mean scheduling time to return phone calls and respond to emails that are not URGENT or LIFE THREATENING. Prioritizing important tasks is essential to remain engaged in this rewarding and challenging profession.

How can you remain the CEO of your day while being pulled in so many directions: administrative duties; supervisions; meetings; mandatory trainings; client needs; crises; travel; and personal life? The following tips will help keep you grounded when the day becomes overwhelming:

1. **You are the CEO of your life!** YOU are 100% responsible for your happiness, your health, wealth, success and the ebb and flow of your day. In this profession, it is easy to succumb to the pressures of the day and feel like a slave to your emails, voicemails, paperwork and even client needs. Being the CEO of your life means taking control of your day consistently. Run the day; do not allow the day to run you.

2. **Monitor the people and things in which you choose to devote energy and time.** Think about the people in your circle. Do they want to see you do well in life? Are they positive? Do they give you constructive feedback? Are they encouraging? If the answer to any of these questions is no, you may want to re-evaluate the reason you choose to allow these people to drain your energy. Think about the people and things that drain the most energy and find ways to minimize and if possible, eliminate them from your life. If they are draining your energy, they are more than likely wasting your time.

3. **Complete the most important task first.** Each day, identify at least 3 tasks that you MUST complete. Complete the most difficult task first. Completing at least one of these tasks at the beginning of the day will put you ahead of schedule.

4. **Rest:** "I'll rest when I'm dead," is a popular statement uttered by many hard workers. I used to live by this statement until I realized how important rest is to be effective in life. I can relate to wanting to squeeze in more work late at night, even when I can barely keep my eyes opened. You may even

punish yourself by not sleeping until you finish that last progress note or complete an assignment. We try to do it all. We help our clients, take care of our families, run businesses, exercise, eat healthy and maintain a positive attitude. This can be exhausting. Since we completed the most important tasks for the day, make a list of important tasks for the next day and go to bed. How effective can you be if you are exhausted? Think of your rest time as intermittently disengaging from the day in order to passionately re-engage the next day.

When asked why people chose this field, the most popular answer remains, "I love helping people." This is a very honorable answer. Let's examine the definition of help. According to Webster's Dictionary, help is defined as doing something that makes it easier for someone to do a job, deal with a problem, aid or assist someone, make something less severe, make something more pleasant or easier to deal with, to give (yourself or another person) food or drink. Most of us attempt to offer our help according to this definition. We offer our help with the best of intentions. We know what our clients need. We know what they should and should not do. We know what works and what does not work. The biggest problem with help that is often overlooked is sometimes help hurts. As helping professionals, we can hurt our clients by imposing our services without asking how they would like to be helped, how they perceive help and their experiences with help in the past. Think about the last time you devoted energy and time into creating a plan or goals *for* a client, instead of discussing *with* them. In most cases, clients may go along with *your* plan because they perceive you as the authority and do not want to disappoint you. After some time passes, you recognize the rhythm has changed. You observe no progress has occurred as well as an increase in cancellations and no-shows. *Your* plan and *your* goals probably factored into this behavior. There will be rare cases where clients will challenge your plan and your goals because they are YOUR goals and not the agreed upon goals between the client and the professional. When we invest the time and energy with our clients by getting curious about how they would like to be helped and the goals they would like to set for themselves, we will save ourselves time from chasing clients who are not interested in a dictator professional relationship with us.

Most of us chose this profession because we are selfless and passionate about effecting positive changes in our communities. I've had the pleasure of working alongside some of the most talented, dedicated, compassionate and hard-working helping professionals. I truly believe that each helping professional has the honorable mission of helping from a genuine place and sometimes the chosen method is a bit flawed. Unfortunately, these flawed methods can be costly. The flawed methods of poor time and energy management can result in professional burnout, compassion fatigue, and clients not getting the help they need. When we mismanage time and energy, this profession can consume us and our souls will pay the price. This work can be mentally draining even when you figure out how to effectively manage your energy and time. As any helping professional reading this book knows, each day will be different and each client will be different. The beautiful thing about effective time and energy management is you do not have to do it all, especially in one day. Take a break and disconnect as needed without feeling guilty. You are no good to yourself or your clients if you are constantly in a mental crisis. Remember, intermittently disengaging from our work is what allows us to passionately re-engage. You deserve it. Your clients deserve it.

The following assessments will assist you in evaluating the management of your time and energy, connect the dots in areas you are feeling stuck and assist you in capitalizing on the areas in your life that deserve maximum time and energy.

**Energy Management**
Identify at least 3 people in your circle who inspire you or encourage you to be better.

_____

_____

_____

*Circle the answer that applies to you.*

Do you have a mentor?

Yes or No

My best effort never feels like enough.

Always    Most of the Time    Sometimes    Never

I can count on my support system.

Always    Most of the Time    Sometimes    Never

I have a hard time relaxing.

Always    Most of the Time    Sometimes    Never

**Time Management**

How much time do you spend working per week? ___

Time spent actively doing work per week_____

Time spent thinking about work per week_____

Time spent commuting for work per week_____

Time spent planning for work per week_____

How much time do you spent per week with your family? _____

How much time do you spend per week on personal development? (reading, attending seminars, classes, audios)_____

How much time do you devote to some form of physical exercise? (walking, running, aerobics, strength training)

_____

_____
_____.

What is the first thing you do when you wake up in the morning?

_____
_____
_____.

What is the first thing you do when you come home from work?

_____
_____
_____.

**Boundary Management**
Do you have scheduled time to check emails?
Yes or No

When there is conflict in your professional and personal life, which area consistently takes preference?

_____
_____
_____.

Do you use all your vacation days?
Yes or No

Do you use sick time when you are sick?
Yes or No

Do you set aside time to eat lunch during the work day?

Yes or No

Do you respond to client messages on your days off? (Does not apply if you are on-call)

Yes or No

# CHAPTER SEVEN

## WHO HELPS THE HELPER?

*"You yourself as much as anyone in the entire universe deserve love and affection."* ~Buddha

After a day of meeting with numerous clients to administer mental or physical healing, someone asks about your day. You find yourself almost too exhausted to speak and respond, "They feel better, but I don't."

Self-care is not a luxury but a priority as well as a necessity in the work we do. From a professional standpoint, we give so much of ourselves so often that it becomes second nature. In a given day, most helping professionals are in various settings (community, office, school, hospital, government agencies) offering their services and advocating for the needs of their clients. After managing these daily responsibilities, most of us are expected to be on call. In case you have not experienced the life of an on-call helping professional, allow me to explain. While on call, you do not work traditional business hours; you are ALWAYS on the clock! You are responsible for the physical and emotional well-being of those you serve. It is difficult for most to rest during this time as one's senses are more heightened while being charged with the incredible responsibility of managing mental health and/or medical crises.

I can recall my first encounter as an on-call mental health therapist. I was responsible for managing the mental health crises of children and families after business hours. My biggest fear was experiencing a client committing suicide. A wise mentor gave me frightening but helpful and career-changing advice that forced me to grow up in this field. I was told to expect it. This advice may sound harsh or familiar depending on where you are in your career. It resonated with me as I was equipped with the skills and compassion to manage suicidal crises. The on-call crisis worker must possess a unique set of skills and patience to attend to their daily crises and then transition to the crises that occur after business hours. Oftentimes, when these after hour crises occur, the worker may be spending time with their family or sleeping. By now, you are probably thinking, "This is what you signed up for." I agree that if you are in the helping profession, you DID sign up for this and you should not be robbed of work-life balance for your choice. There are also consequences for failing to practice good self-care.

One of the most common conditions experienced by helping professionals who fail to practice good self-care is compassion fatigue, also known as burnout, secondary traumatic stress or vicarious traumatization. It is characterized by a gradual lessening of compassion over time. This condition is common in direct line workers or first responders such as EMT's, nurses, doctors, social workers, case managers, counselors and psychologists. There is evidence that compassion fatigue increases when helping professionals do not see individuals getting better.

## How do I know if I am experiencing compassion fatigue?

### *Recognize the signs!*

In recognizing the signs, reflect on the baseline of your emotions, energy, sleep patterns, appetite and socialization.

- *Do you feel exhausted even after getting more than six hours of sleep each night?*
- *Do you consistently have difficulty falling and/or staying asleep at night?*
- *Do you find yourself consistently dreading meeting with clients?*
- *Do you consistently struggle with being present in sessions with clients?*
- *Do you find yourself consistently desensitizing from the trauma experienced by your clients?*
- *Are you having nightmares of the trauma experienced by your clients?*
- *Have you given up hope on your ability to help your clients make positive changes?*
- *Do you consistently become anxious when thinking about work?*
- *Have you noticed an extreme increase or decrease in your appetite?*

**If you answered yes to 4 or more questions, I highly recommend that you seek the self-care options (which may include seeking professional help) that I will discuss in the next section.**

Other red flags include:
- Anger
- Blaming
- Chronic lateness
- Depression
- Diminished sense of personal accomplishments
- Irritability
- Gastrointestinal complaints
- Physical and mental exhaustion
- Frequent headaches

So, the question remains, "Who helps the helper?"

How can I practice good self-care while meeting the needs of clients as well as the many demands of this profession?

- **Be your own advocate:** Taking care of your mental health should be a priority especially in the current climate of large caseloads, high turnover rates and great public pressure. We are the best advocates for our clients and oftentimes fail to advocate for our own needs. When is the last time you advocated for a lighter caseload, increase in pay, time off, support or transparency from upper management? Be the change you want to see by modeling to the communities you serve the importance of advocating for yourself.

- **Know your limits.** Set boundaries with your clients. This means not taking calls after business hours (after ensuring that they know who to call in the event of crisis). If you are one who feels compelled to answer the phone after hours, turn it off! You are not ignoring your clients; you are modeling boundary setting. Boundaries keep us safe and you will need your energy to continue to help them. It is important for our clients to understand our roles in their lives as professionals. Lines can get blurred because we are giving care and seeing them at their most vulnerable states. However, as a wise woman told me, "You can't be everything to everybody." Set your boundary!

- **Seek Supervision:** You are not alone in this process and you do not have all the answers. Use your supervisor and demand quality supervision. Quality supervision should be a combination of support, education and administrative. Unfortunately, most of us get too comfortable in our routine and neglect the supervision of a more seasoned professional. Some of the benefits of supervision include an objective perspective and a supportive environment. An objective perspective during supervision can assist you in viewing your situation through a different lens, thus shifting from a place of cynicism to a place of empathy. The support of a supervisor is invaluable. Sometimes the role of the supervisor may be to listen to your concerns and encourage (or even direct) you to take time off. Seeking supervision also applies to those professionals running various types of private practices. Supervision is imperative for private practitioners as most are operating solo and wearing many hats, such as but not limited to, practitioner, assistant, accountant, marketing which can lead to burnout or compassion fatigue if not addressed.

- **Breathe:** When you find yourself in a stressful situation, breathe! Take a long, deep breath in and slowly exhale. Breathing calms the reactive part of our brain. It is so automatic, that oftentimes we forget or are unaware of the benefits of taking deep breaths. Deep breathing helps us to find our center.

- **Rest & Recuperation or Relaxation (R&R):** Did you know that 4 of the 10 careers with the highest rates of depression are careers in the helping profession? Per health.com, Nursing home/Child Care Worker tops the list followed by Social Work (4), Heath Care Workers (5)

(Doctors, Nurses, Therapists) and Teachers (7). The reasons cited for the high rates of depression include professionals working long, unpredictable hours, working with people who are not getting better but have a lot of needs, low compensation, high demands and expectations, experiencing trauma, sickness and death daily. Working in a demanding, yet rewarding profession can take its toll on you *if* you fail to take the time you need to recuperate, regroup and disconnect from work. You are no good to those you serve if you are tired, burned out or fatigued.

Many jobs require that we work toward completing tasks and big projects before leaving work. What separates this profession from others is you cannot place a timetable when encouraging one to enhance their life for the better. The helping profession is an ongoing process. At the close of each day, you may need to apply some variation of the following positive affirmation in your routine: "I gave each person my all regardless of the outcome." Remember, we are responsible for helping in the process. The people we serve are responsible for the outcomes of their lives.

You are not a machine. You need time to socialize, relax and exercise. Life is not only about work, the office and your clients. While it may seem like the norm to let work consume you, the purpose of having a work-life balance is that you are striving toward creating balance. This balance can lead to more satisfaction personally and professionally. Professionally, you can do what you love and disconnect from work without the guilt. Personally, you can invest quality time with your loved ones versus squeezing in time as your schedule permits.

Most of us in the helping profession find ourselves burned out in just a few days of returning to work from a week vacation. How do you learn to manage yourself in "the pressure cooker?" The most important thing you can do to sustain yourself is to develop your core principles and values of practice. If you are working for a company, you may want to ask yourself, "Does this company's mission align with my personal mission statement?" If the answer is no, it may be time to re-evaluate your plan. If you are a business owner, you may want to ask yourself, "Is my company equipped to serve our target population?" If not, it may be time to go back to the drawing board to re-evaluate your plan for meeting this need. Or, do you still desire to help this population?

As helping professionals, we get the privilege of having people trust us at their most vulnerable states, and sharing their hearts, minds and lives to us. We are charged with the responsibility to do no harm. A huge part of doing no harm is recognizing when we are burned out and taking action. Sometimes helping is our best and worst quality. Our help can hurt our clients if we are giving from a dry well. There are a lot of withdrawals being deducted from our spirits daily. It is up to us to find ways to make healthy deposits into our souls. This may include seeking help, and that is okay, we are humans and we are not exempt!

# CHAPTER EIGHT

## BE THE BEST VERSION OF YOU

*"When you are living the best version of yourself, you inspire others to live the best version of themselves." ~Steve Maraboli*

Being the best version of you can mean different things for different people. *Vitamin C Healing for the Mind, Body and Soul* taught us being the best version of us encompasses a holistic approach to our lives from a physical, psychological, emotional and spiritual standpoint. As helping professionals, we must embrace this holistic approach to be the best version of ourselves. We must also set strategic intentions to disconnect and transcend into the next session, appointment or meeting with a clear and focused mind. I can empathize with the tight schedules, back-to-back appointments and the pressure of remaining with a client in crisis while your next client is in the waiting area. To give the best version of you, you need time to "reset", to prepare for the next session. Resetting can mean doing something that periodically takes you away from your work area to disconnect. Go for a walk, do a breathing exercise, meditate, say a prayer, drink some coffee, tea, or glass of water. These grounding examples are imperative to help us briefly disengage so we can effectively re-engage with our clients.

Resetting yourself for each client interaction can be challenging due to the quick turnaround between appointments. Many of us may have a difference of opinion on how to reset ourselves. There isn't a right or wrong method to how one resets him or herself.

The important thing is to reset. If this is you, you need to take the extra time out for you. Remember, you are human. You are not a machine. Our clients deserve the best version of us, which includes transparency, authenticity and our presence, not perfection. When you need to reset before the next session, kindly ensure their comfort in the waiting area and have a conversation with your client that you will be with him/her momentarily.

We got into this field because we want to help. Oftentimes, while we are trying to help, we neglect ourselves. You cannot give help from a depleted spiritual account. A lot of withdrawals are taken from your spiritual account each day. You are responsible for making deposits into your spiritual account to maintain balance. Failing to do so can result in an overdrawn spiritual account. Balance your spiritual account daily!

What matters the most to you will be revealed in the life lessons you consider the most important. Being the best version of you may require you to go through your own healing process.

The following reflection questions will allow you to process where you are in this journey.

Who are you at your best?

_____

_____

_____.

Identify an area in your practice in which you struggle. List the steps you plan to take to improve.

_____

_____

_____.

What do you believe are the top 3 strengths you possess as a helping professional?

_____

_____

_____.

What values drive your decision making when attempting to address a client's issue?

_____

_____

_____.

What has been your most significant contribution to the helping profession?

_____

_____

_____.

What change do you want to make in the world?

_____

_____

_____.

Being the best version of you takes a lot of self-reflection, which may be uncomfortable for many of us. I challenge you to take at least 7 days and observe yourself. Observe your actions, habits and triggers. What makes you happy? What inspires you? What drains you? How do you respond to crises? How do your respond to change? How do you respond to conflict? How do you spend most of your time?

Never stop learning because life never stops teaching. Be the best version of you, unapologetically. Everyone else is taken.

# BONUS CHAPTER

**DO I DARE…**
**TO BECOME THE BEST VERSION OF ME**

**BOOK OF INSPIRATIONS**

## BOOK OF INSPIRATIONS

Do you find yourself daydreaming about a passion you have yet to pursue? Are you stuck existing in your daily routine instead of living or walking in your purpose? Do you know changes need to be made in your life, but fear what resides on the other side of change? Are you ready to get unstuck? There is a common myth that it takes 21-30 days to form a new habit. A recent study published in the European Journal of Social Psychology examined the habits of 96 people over a 12-week period.

The results revealed it takes from 18-254 days for people to form a new habit and more than 2 months, 66 days to be exact, before a new behavior becomes automatic.

Do I Dare, Book of Inspirations includes 66 daily inspirational quotes that will invite you to step out of your comfort zone, tap into your greatness, and inspire you as you work toward making lasting changes, forming healthy and more adaptive automatic habits in any facet of your life.

**Day 1:** "Don't compare your beginning to someone else's middle. Everything that you will ever be is already inside of you."

**Day 2:** "Tough times can be more readily endured if we remain convicted."

**Day 3:** "Failure is a prerequisite to success. It is success turned inside out. The most successful people have failed before succeeding."

**Day 4:** "We cannot become who we aspire to be by remaining who we are. Every next level of your life will demand a different level of you."

**Day 5:** "Dreams don't work unless you do. The dream is free, but the hustle is sold separately."

**Day 6:** "Fear is only conquered by action. The longer fear is left unattended, the stronger it becomes. Be a verb, take action."

**Day 7:** "The comfort zone is a beautiful and relaxing place, but nothing grows there. When you step out of your comfort zone, you are stepping into greatness. Life truly begins outside of your comfort zone. Get comfortable with being uncomfortable."

**Day 8:** "Your life is too important to straddle the fence of indecision. Indecision in our relationships, careers, health and businesses will cost us dearly in the long run. You cannot make progress without making decisions. Indecision is the thief of opportunity."

**Day 9:** "You cannot change what is going on around you until you change what is going on within you. Be the change you want to see in the world."

**Day 10:** "Do not wait another moment to go back to school, start a business, apologize, say I love you, live a healthier lifestyle, be a better mate, be a better parent. There is no such thing as a perfect moment. The time is now!

**Day 11:** "Strive for progress in being the best version of you, not perfection."

**Day 12:** "In order to win in life, you must do more than try your best and hope for the best. You must plan to win, prepare to win and most importantly EXPECT to win! You were born to be a winner in life...time to unleash that beast!"

**Day 13:** "The most important decision about your goals is not what you are willing to do to achieve them, but what are you willing to sacrifice? If you do not sacrifice for your goals, your goals will be the sacrifice."

**Day 14:** "What a privilege it is to be alive! You will never have this day again...make it count!"

**Day 15:** "Keep pushing! What seems tough today will be your "warm up" one day!"

**Day 16:** "You are the sum of your five closest friends. Either your circle is inspiring you to be the best version of you or sabotaging your efforts to be the best version of you."

**Day 17:** "Distractions destroy action. It is nearly impossible to do big things when you are distracted by small things. Starve those distractions and feed your focus."

**Day 18:** "If it does not align with your purpose, walk away!"

**Day 19:** "Patience + Persistence = Perseverance!"

**Day 20:** "Take the action today that will move you toward achieving your goals. Remember, desire loses its value without a sense of urgency."

**Day 21:** "You can have excuses or you can have results, but you cannot have both."

**Day 22:** "Be bigger than your excuses! Do not let your reason "why not" be bigger than your reason "why!""

**Day 23:** "Stay true to your vision and embrace your unique journey. What GOD has for you is for you!"

**Day 24:** "If you want to get more out of life, you must

be willing to give more to life. Never take more out of life than you intend to give back, even when you know you may get nothing in return."

**Day 25:** "Build a solid foundation and see it through with integrity. Success without integrity is failure."

**Day 26:** "Find your voice, then give yourself permission to use your voice."

**Day 27:** "Don't run away from your fears! Your fears are not there to scare you, but to remind you that what you fear most is worth fighting for. Lean into your fears, embrace your fears and create certainty in the face of your fears. Feel the fear and do it anyway!"

**Day 28:** "Having unrealistic expectations of people lead to disappointments. Learn to accept people for who they are, not what you want them to be."

**Day 29:** "Approach your daily goals with a non-negotiable mindset. Be willing to do what most people are not willing to do in order to have what most people do not have."

**Day 30:** "The only way out of a challenging situation is through it. You must go through to grow through."

**Day 31:** "Your name is your brand. Your brand is the conversation people have about you when you are not in the room. Protect your good name."

**Day 32:** "One of the most important keys to success is having the discipline to do what you know you should do, even when you do not feel like doing it. Discipline, not desire, determines our destiny."

**Day 33:** "As your journey continues and life conveniently happens, tap into the energy that got you this far. No matter what happens, don't quit. When you're tired…grind! When it's tough…fight! When you win…stay humble!"

**Day 34:** "Success occurs when opportunity meets preparation."

**Day 35:** "Action always beats intention. Actions prove who we are and words prove who we want to be."

**Day 36:** "You cannot be an authority without putting in the work to gain the knowledge."

**Day 37:** "With great power comes great responsibility. The measure of a great man or woman is what he or she chooses to do with this power."

**Day 38:** "When choosing between sacrifice and instant gratification, choose the road less traveled and choose sacrificing your short-term pleasures. Short term sacrifices for long-term success."

**Day 39:** "Learn to hear yourself. Find clarity and find what feels true."

**Day 40:** "Pay it forward with your unobtrusive acts of selflessness and kindness."

**Day 41:** "Don't be a hoarder of knowledge. Each one, teach one."

**Day 42:** "Life is a marathon and not a sprint. Train for endurance, not speed. Quitting will not speed up the process."

**Day 43:** "Opportunity knocks once. It is not about how much the opportunity will cost you, but what it will cost you if you don't answer the door."

**Day 44:** "Adversity reveals character."

**Day 45:** "The best way to get something done is to begin. Procrastination is the cousin of fear, the thief of time and a huge form of self-sabotage."

**Day 46:** "Raise the bar higher! Set a goal so big that you must grow into that person in order to achieve it!"

**Day 47:** "Today marks the start of a new day. Do not dwell on the past, for the past is a place of reference, not a place of residence. Focus on the things with your control, the present and the future."

**Day 48:** "Not everyone will understand your journey. It's not their journey to make sense of…It's yours!"

**Day 49:** "Having the talent, creativity, knowledge and skillset are irrelevant without the mindset to complement. Your mindset creates your skillset."

**Day 50:** "Keep your end in mind."

**Day 51:** "You can handle whatever today throws at you!"

**Day 52:** "Don't forget to celebrate your small successes. Each success is a win. Get used to winning!"

**Day 53:** "If it is going to be, it is up to me."

**Day 54:** "It won't be easy, but it will be worth it. If it were easy, everybody would be doing it."

**Day 55:** "Life is tough but so are you. You are stronger than you think."

**Day 56:** "What consumes your mind controls your life. If you dwell on problems, you will have more problems. If you focus on successes, you will have more success."

**Day 57:** "Set a goal so big that you can't achieve it until you grow into the person who can." ~Unknown

**Day 58:** "Run the day; don't let the day run you. You are the CEO of your life!"

**Day 59:** "Have an attitude of gratitude. There is always something to be thankful for."

**Day 60:** "Turn your 'I can't' into an 'I can' and your dreams into goals."

**Day 61:** "Your only competition is being better than you were yesterday."

**Day 62:** "What worries you owns you. Worrying will never change the outcome!"

**Day 63:** "Work more on yourself than you do your job. The Return on Investment on personal development is invaluable."

**Day 64:** "The struggle of life is inevitable. You can be a victim of your struggles or a victor of your struggles."

**Day 65:** "Discipline your disappointments!"

**Day 66:** "Your life is your legacy to the world. You get to decide what legacy you leave behind."

# ABOUT THE AUTHOR

Sharise M. Nance has more than 16 years of experience in the helping profession. Mrs. Nance is a Licensed Clinical Social Worker, Certified Clinical Trauma Professional, award winning author. She has presented keynotes and seminars nationally for young professionals, entrepreneurs, parents and adolescents. She has also been featured on local TV shows, newspapers, magazines and national podcasts. Mrs. Nance is the co-owner and co-founder of HandinHand Counseling Services, LLC, a private counseling practice dedicated to promoting HOPE, HEALTH, and HEALING to individuals and families dealing with generational and situational obstacles. Sharise enjoys traveling, watching sports, exercising and spending time with her family. She resides in Pittsburgh, PA, with her husband William Nance.

### Stay Connected with Sharise
www.vitaminchealing.com or www.hihcounseling.com
Email: VitaminCHealing@gmail.com
Facebook: www.facebook.com/VitaminChealing
Twitter: www.twitter.com/HopeHealthHeal
### Other Works by Sharise
Vitamin C: Healing for the Mind, Body and Soul
Vitamin C: The Healing Workbook
Available at Amazon.com, VitaminCHealing.com and
www.EX3Books.com

www.ingramcontent.com/pod-product-compliance
Lightning Source LLC
Chambersburg PA
CBHW060554100426
42742CB00013B/2559